Adult Coloring Book

Stress Relieving Horse Designs

By Infinity Coloring Books

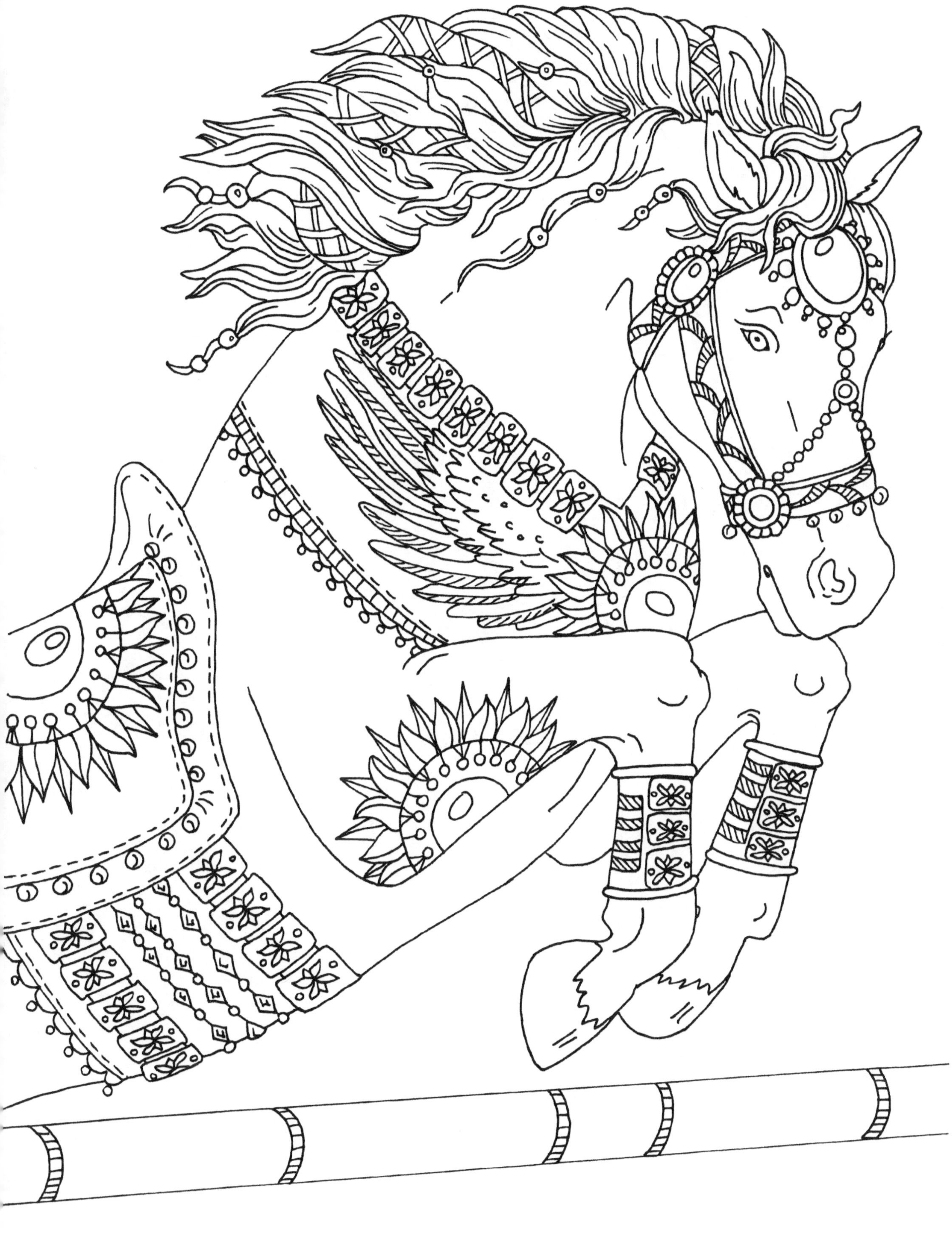

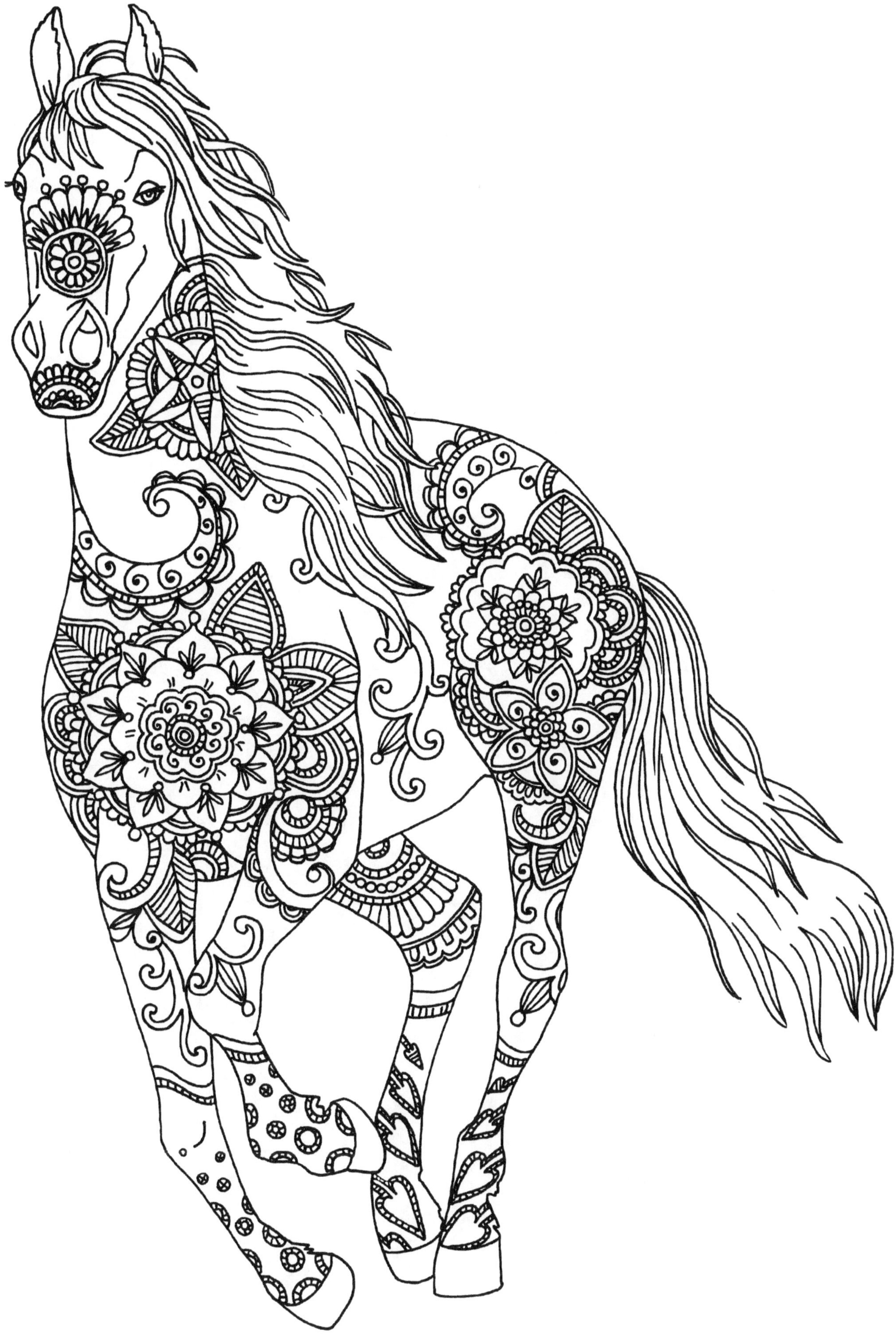

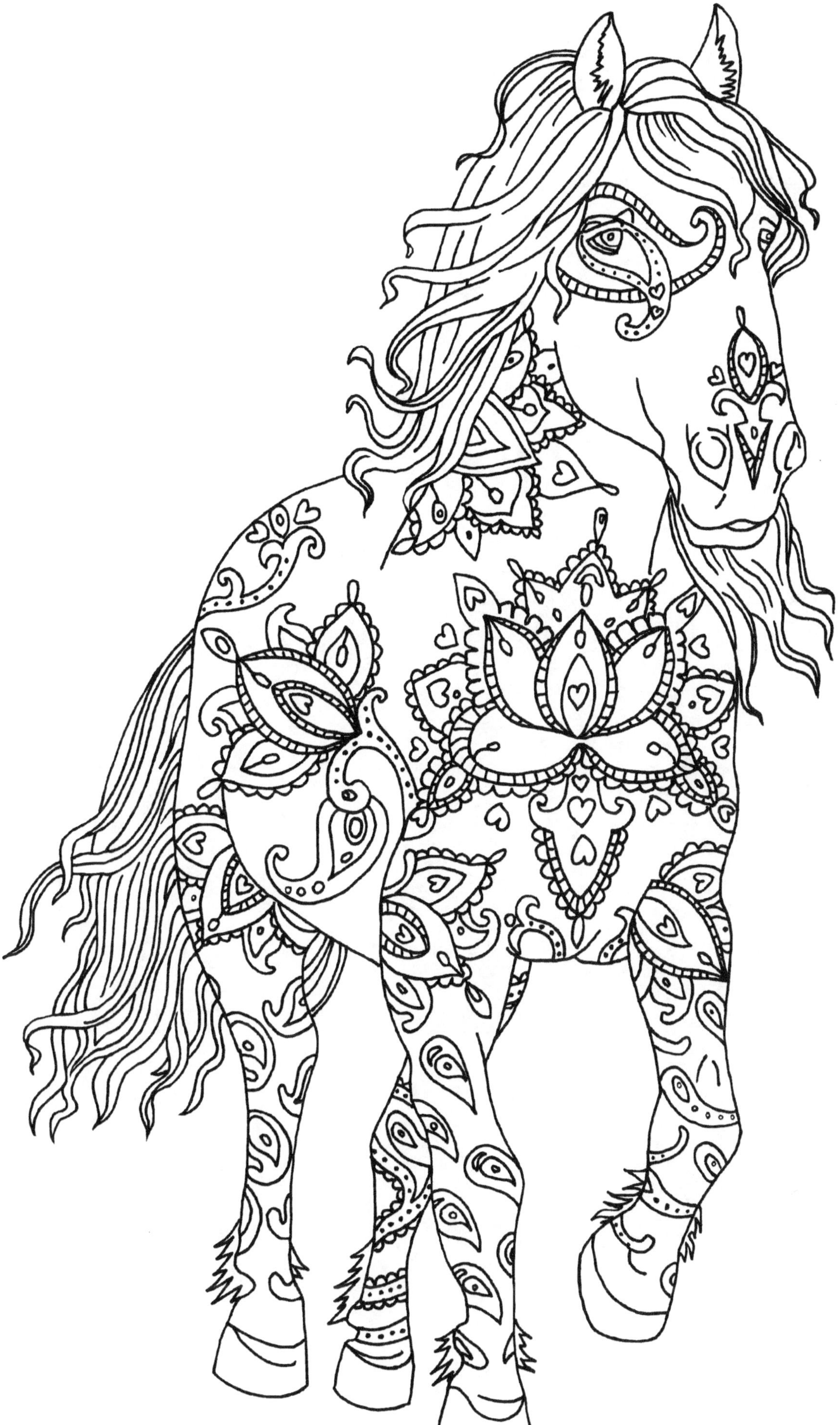

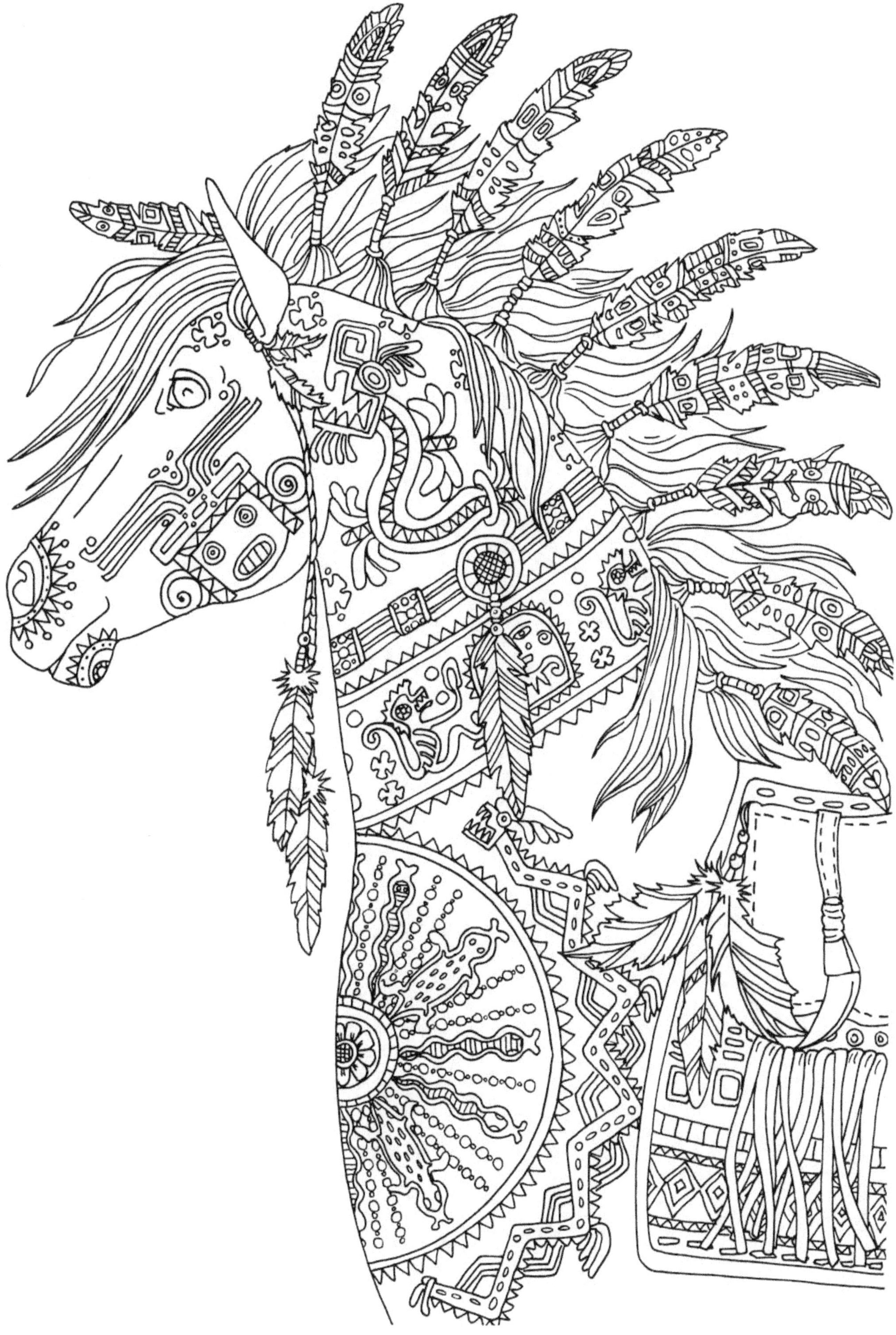

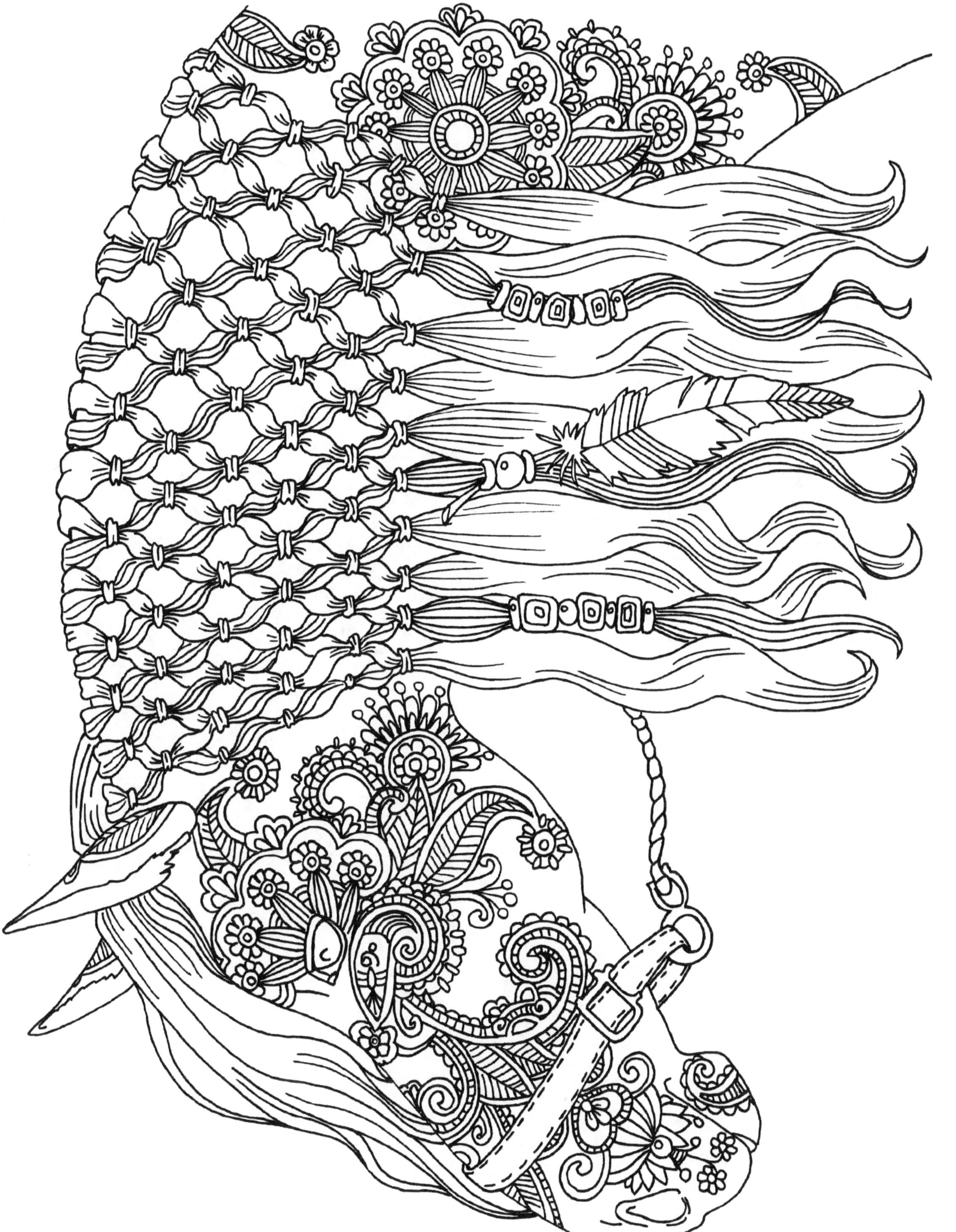

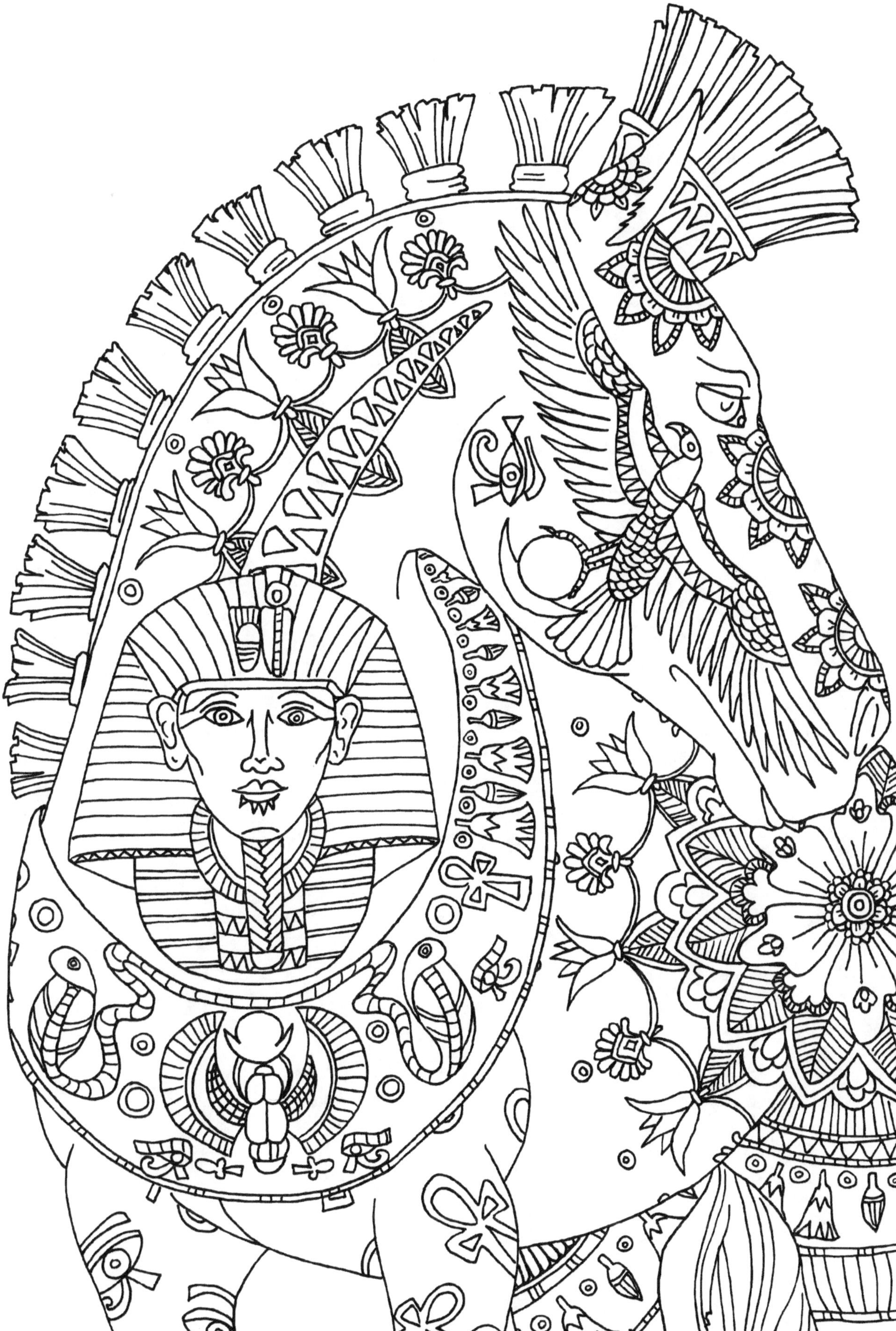

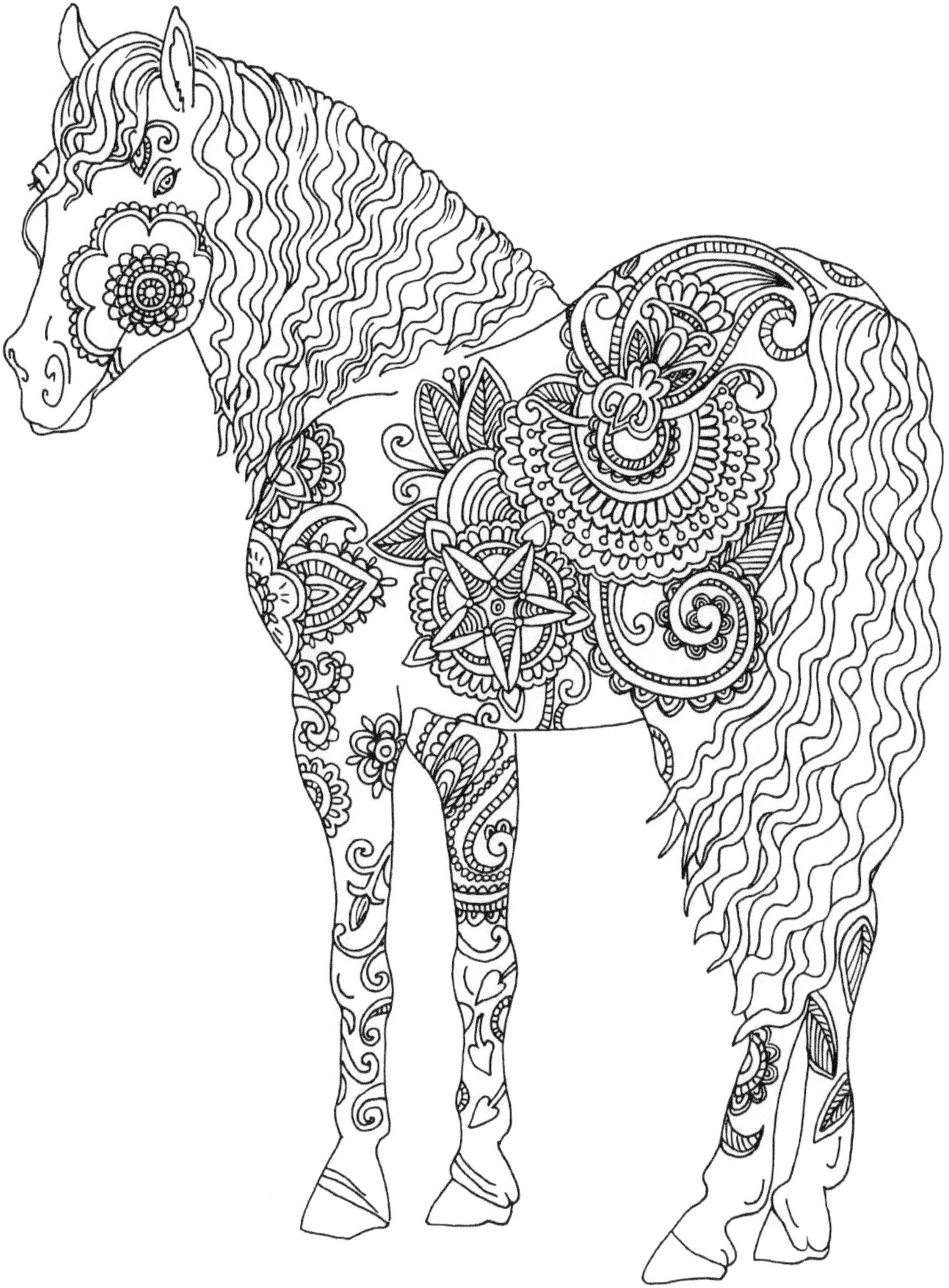

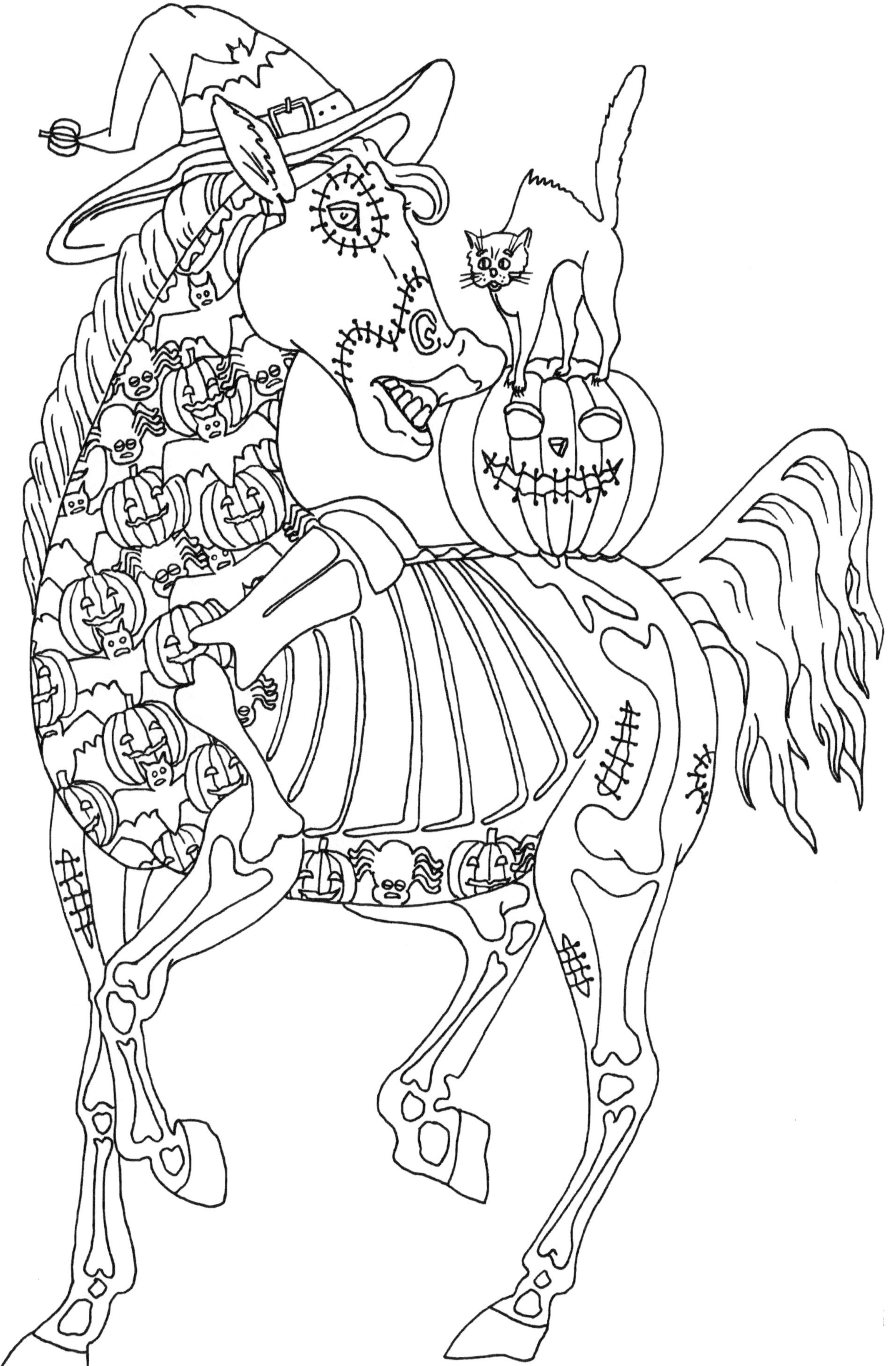

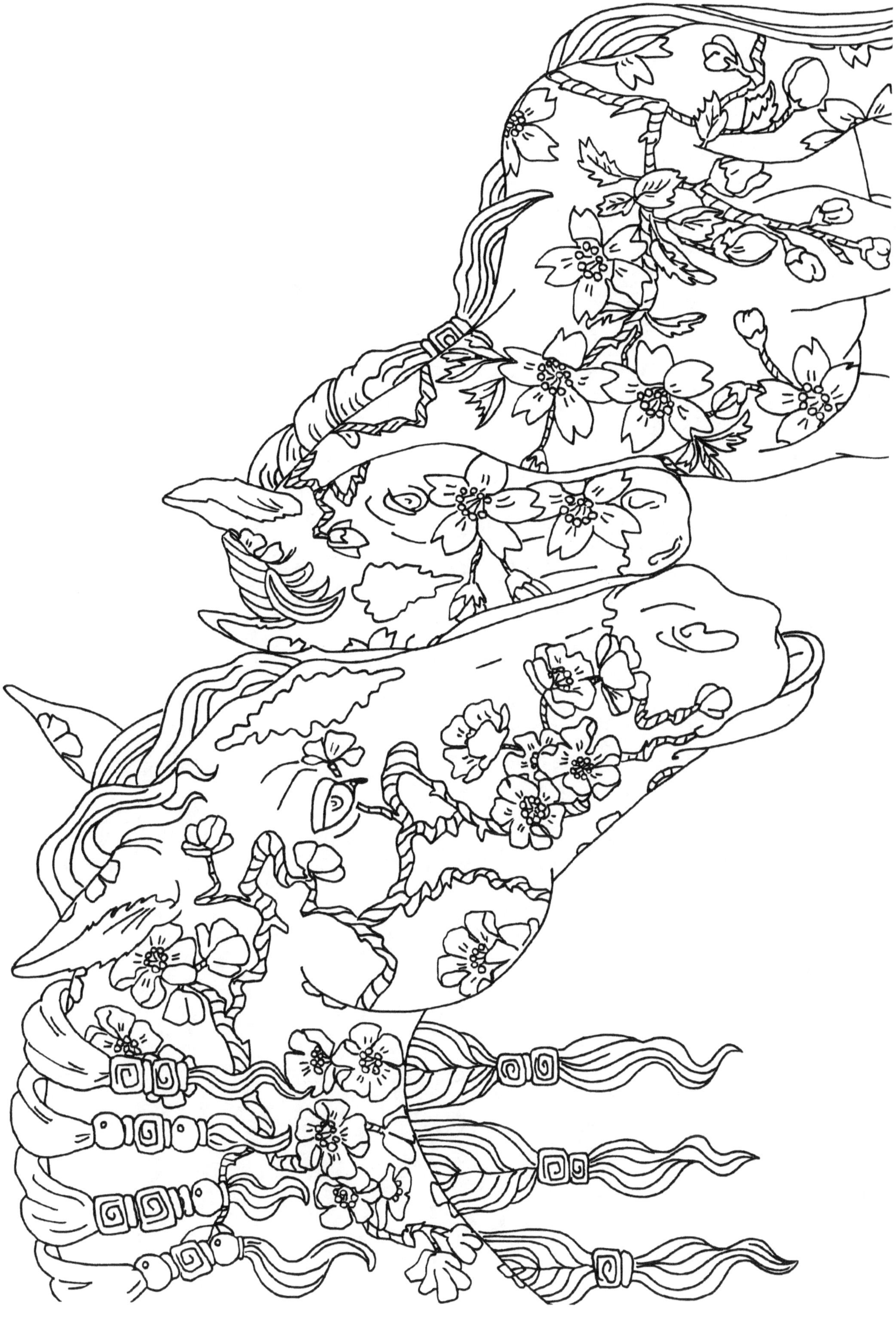

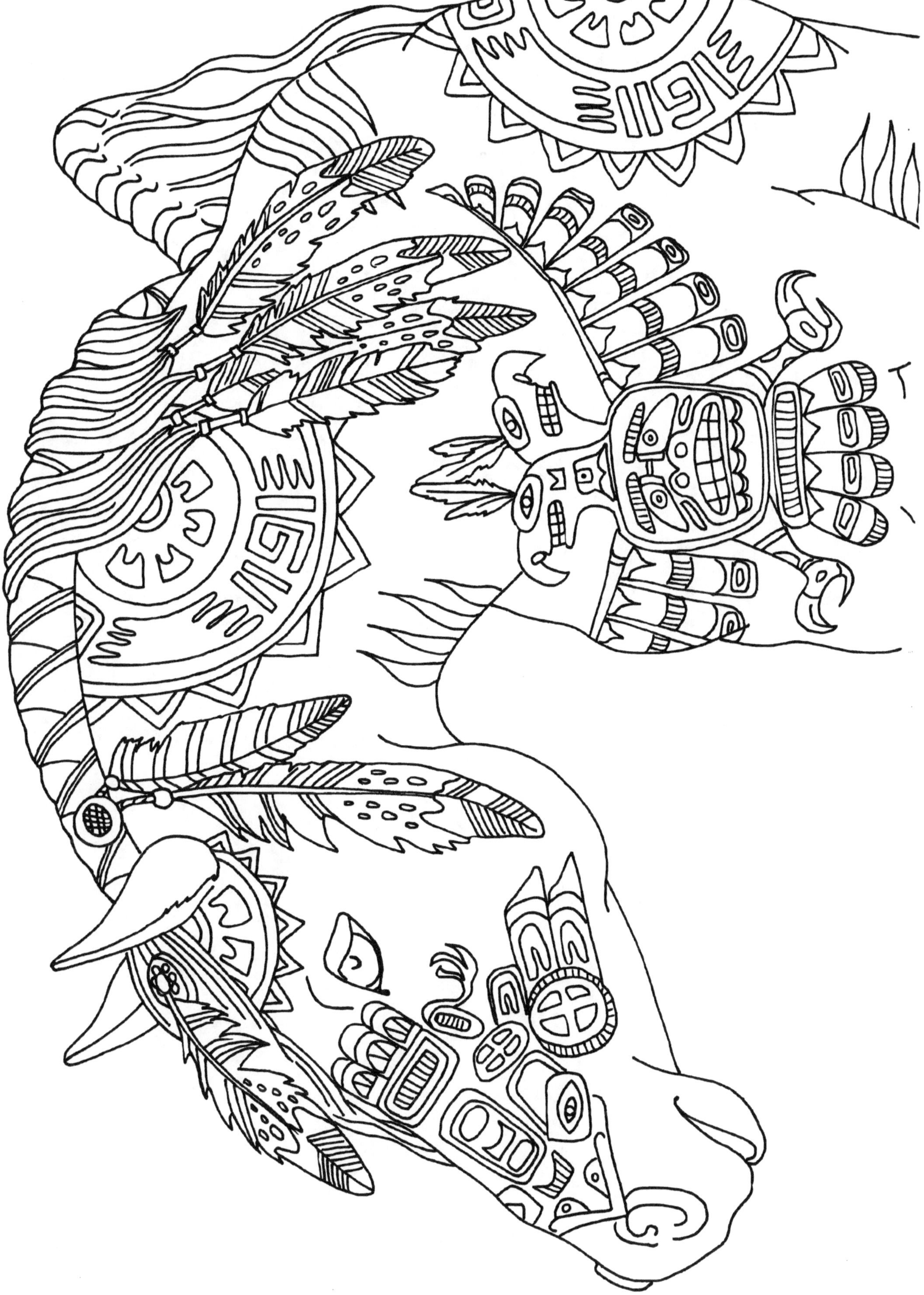

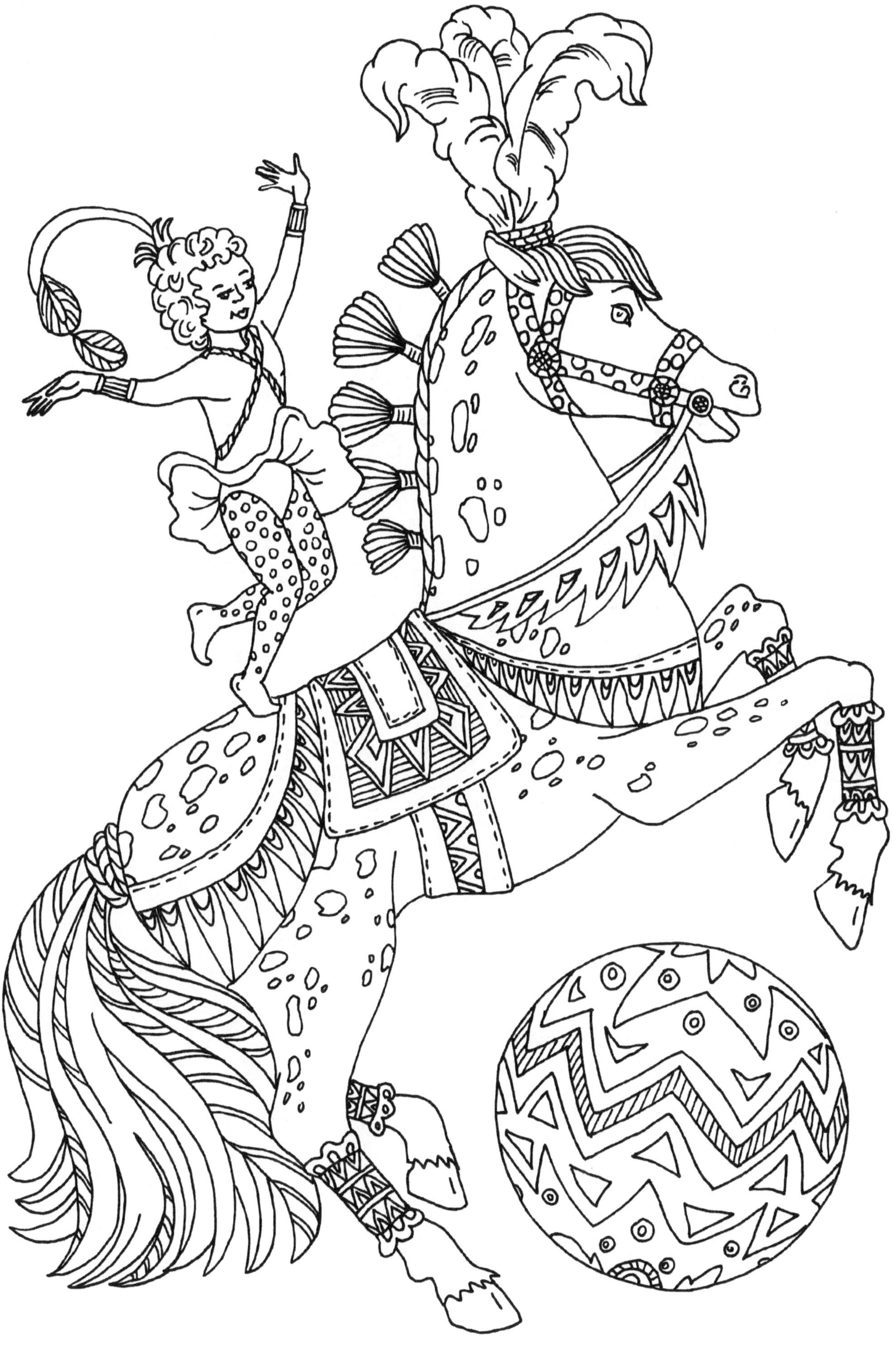

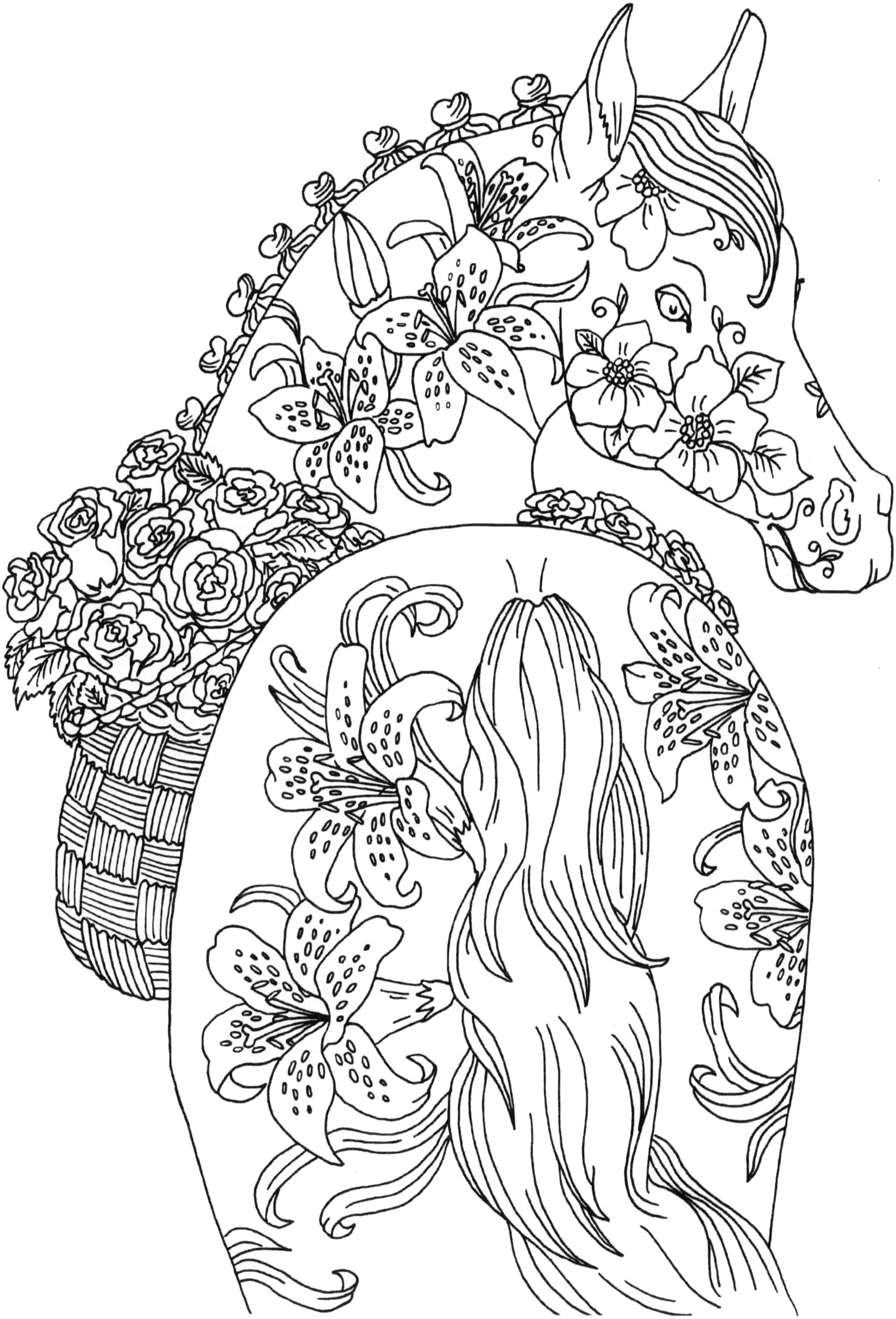

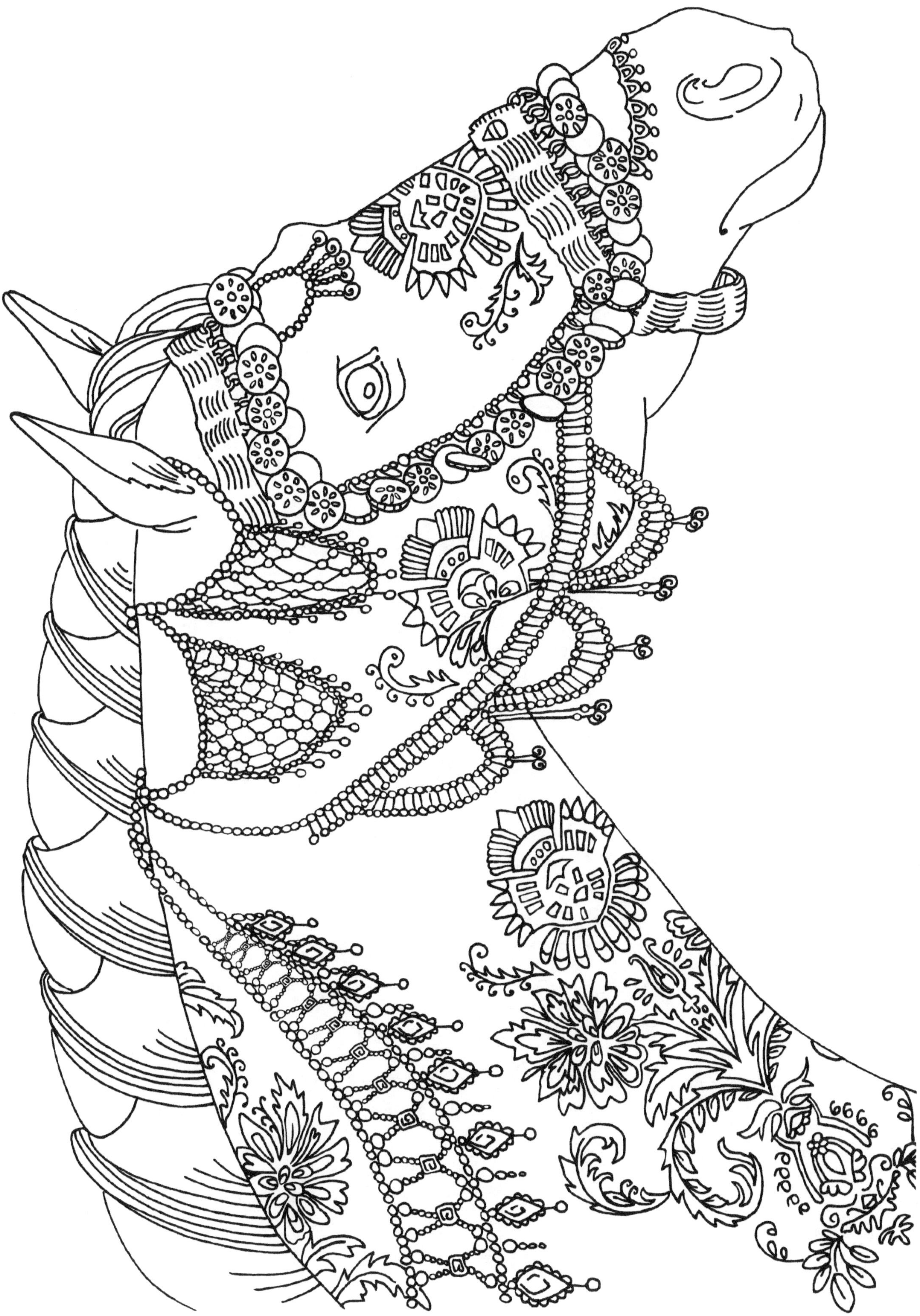

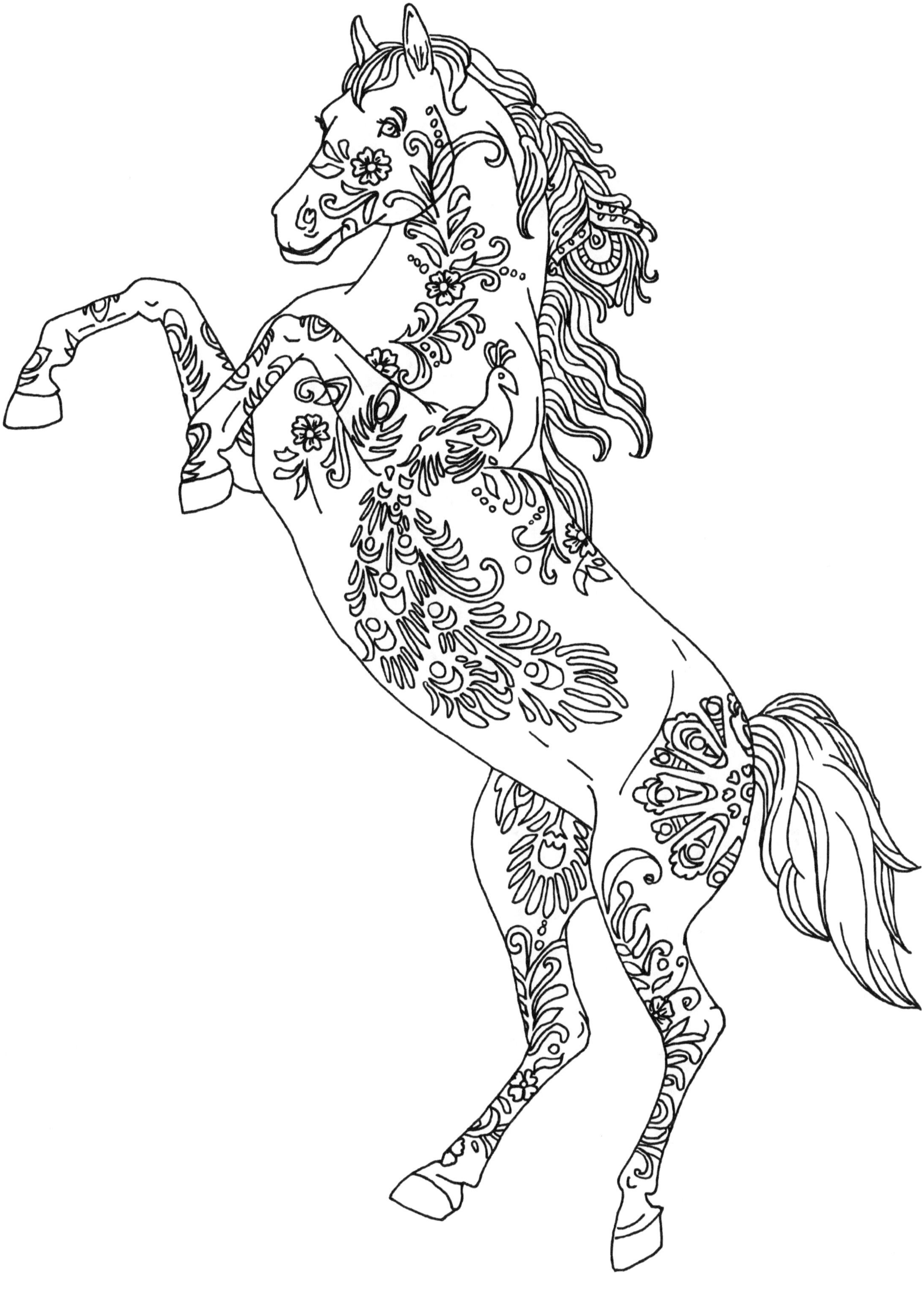

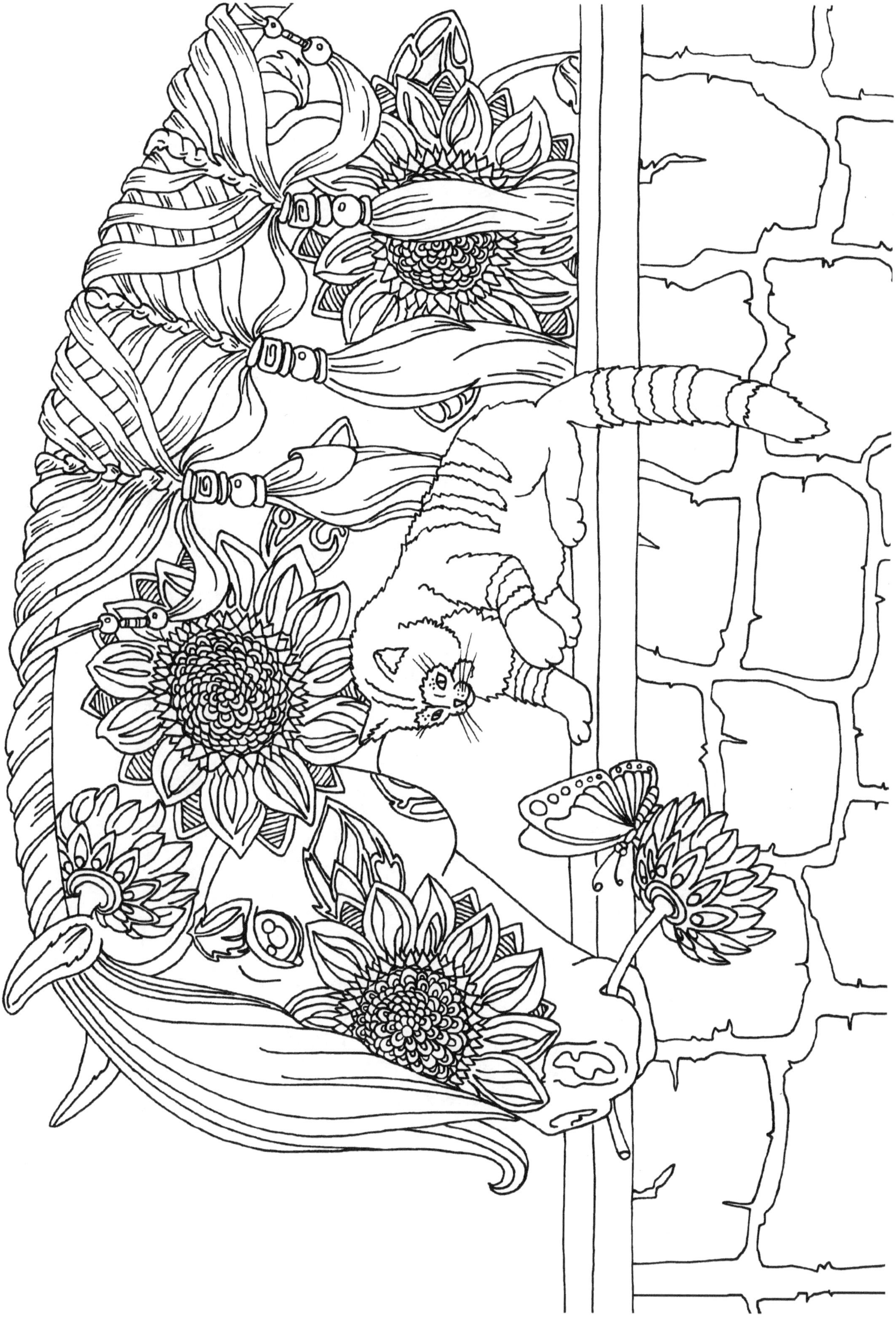

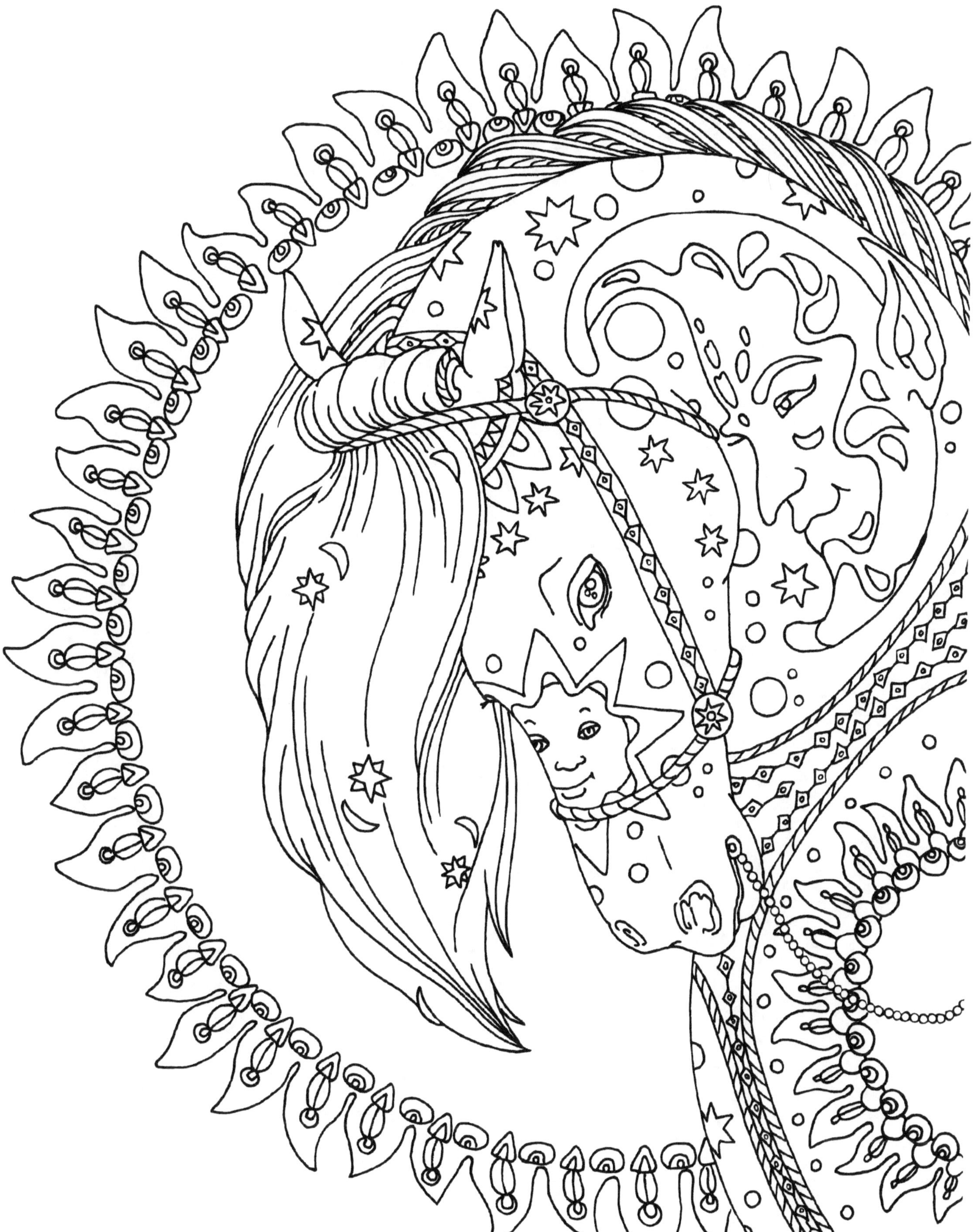

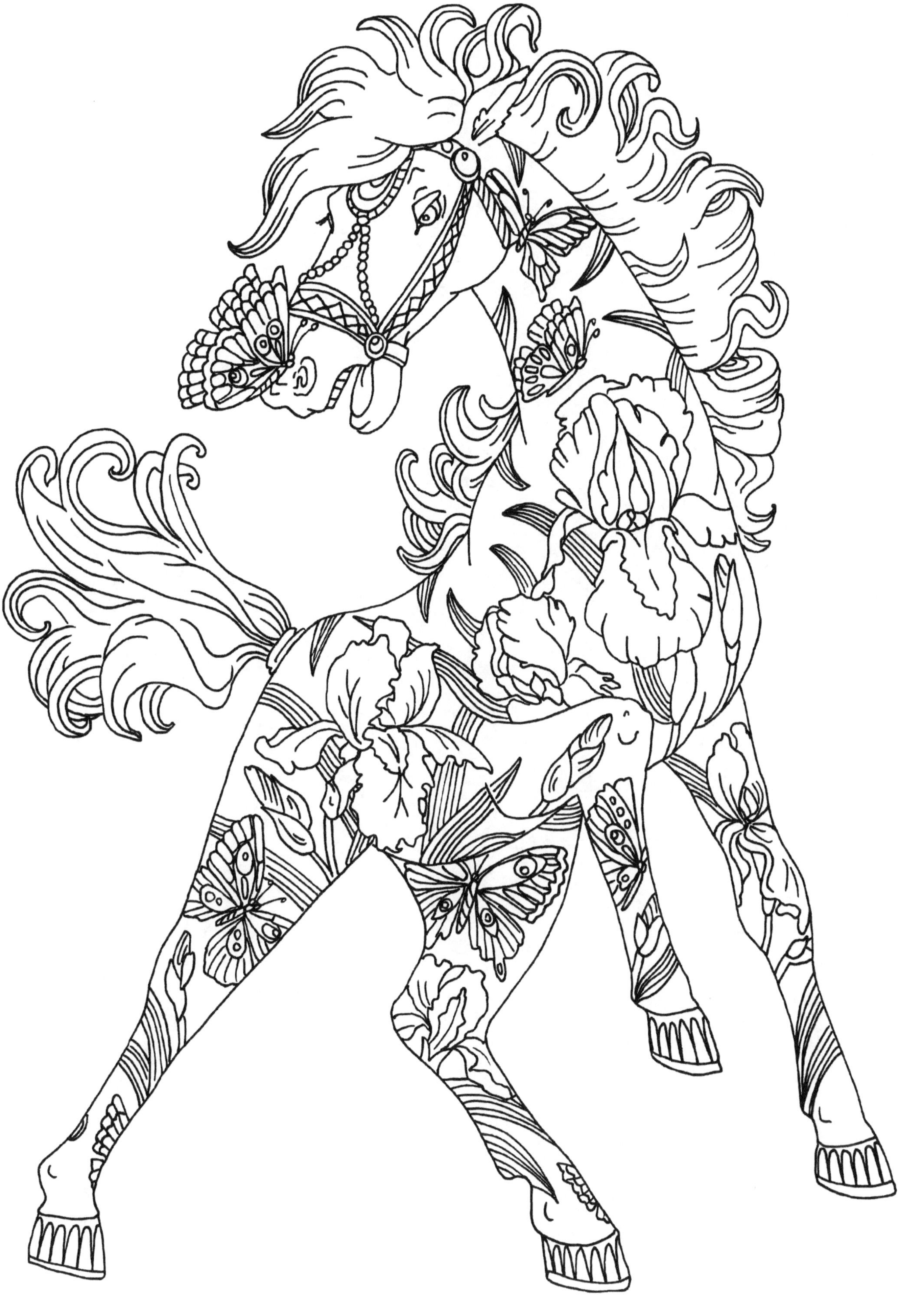

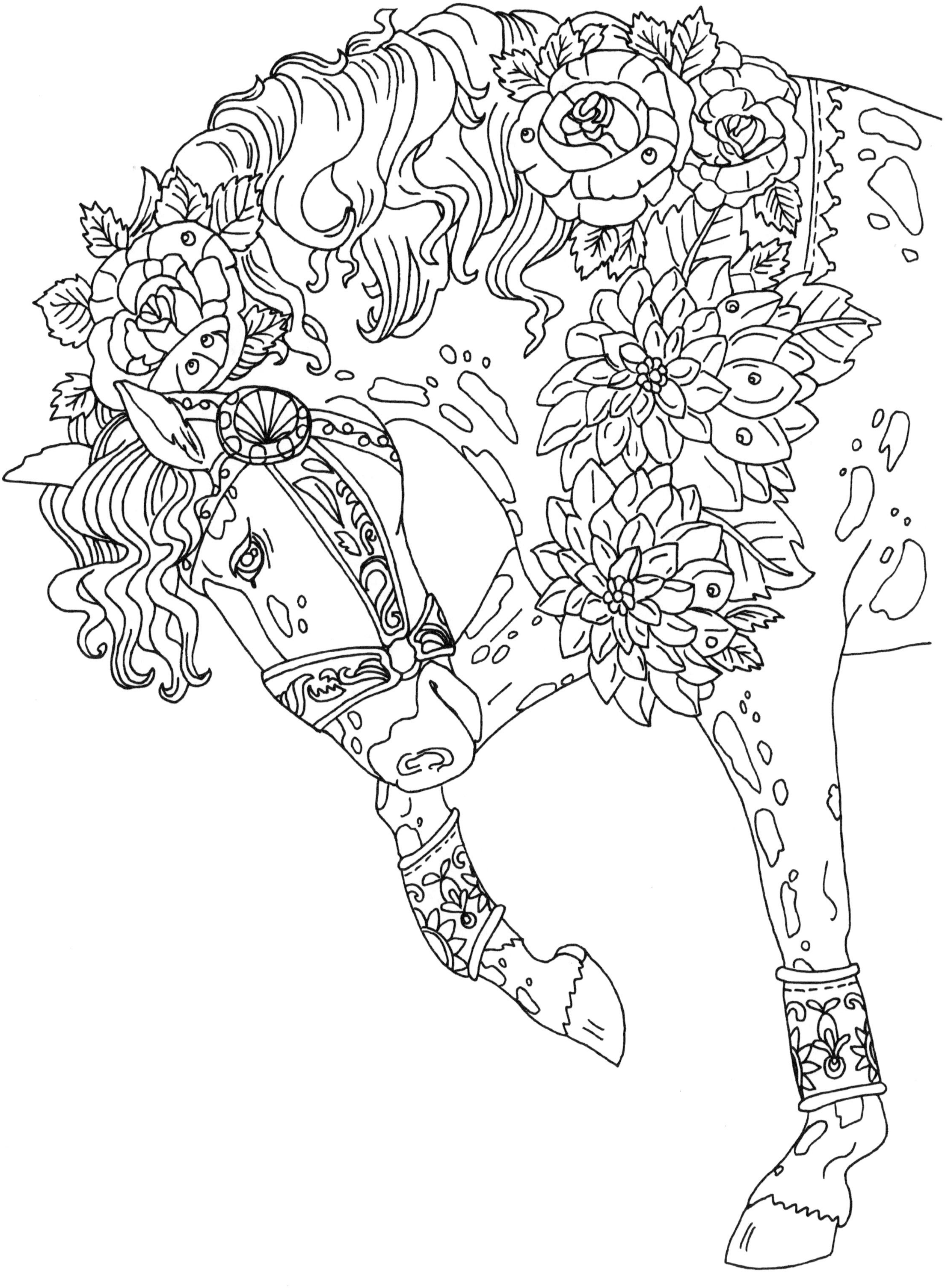

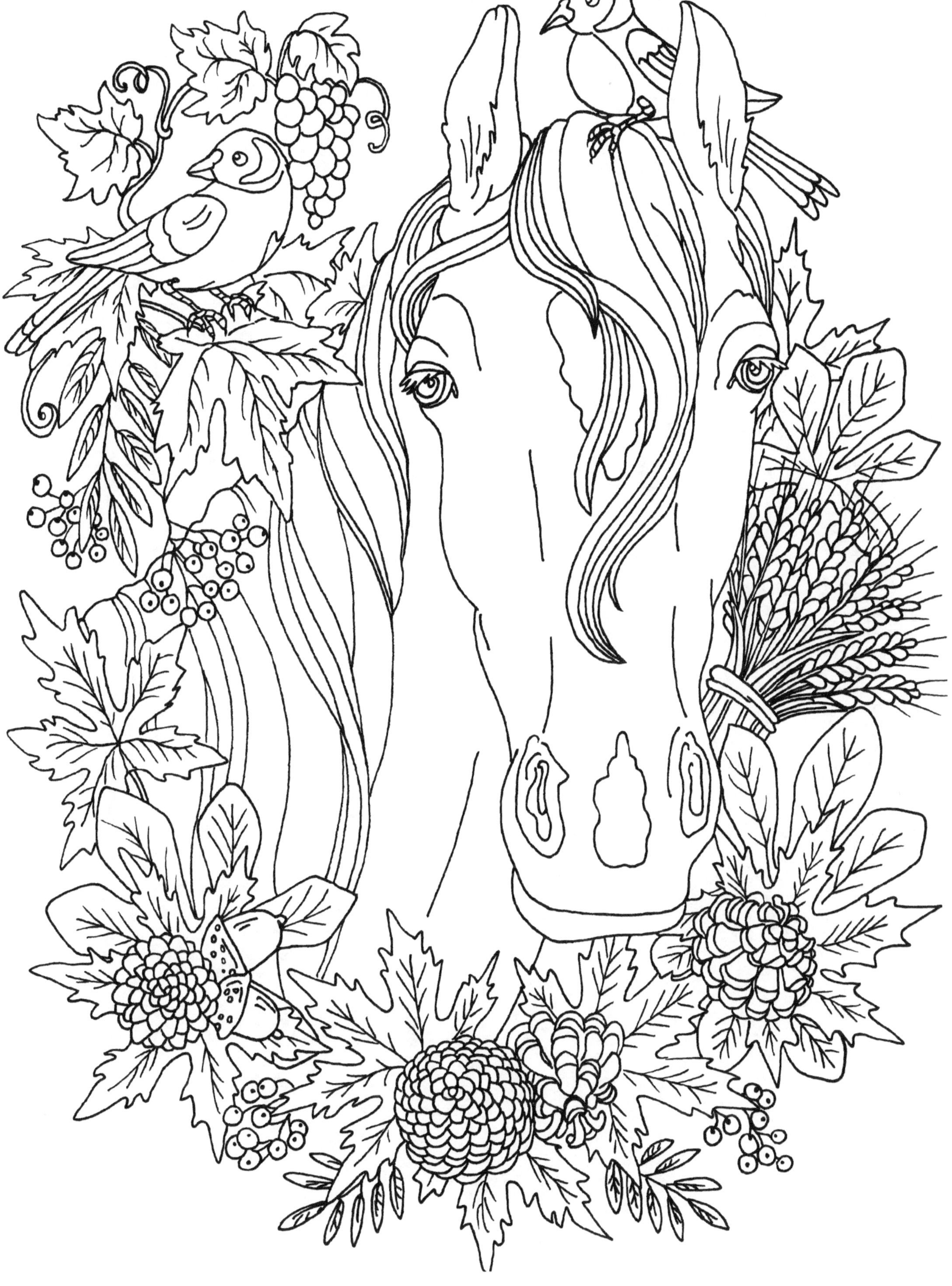

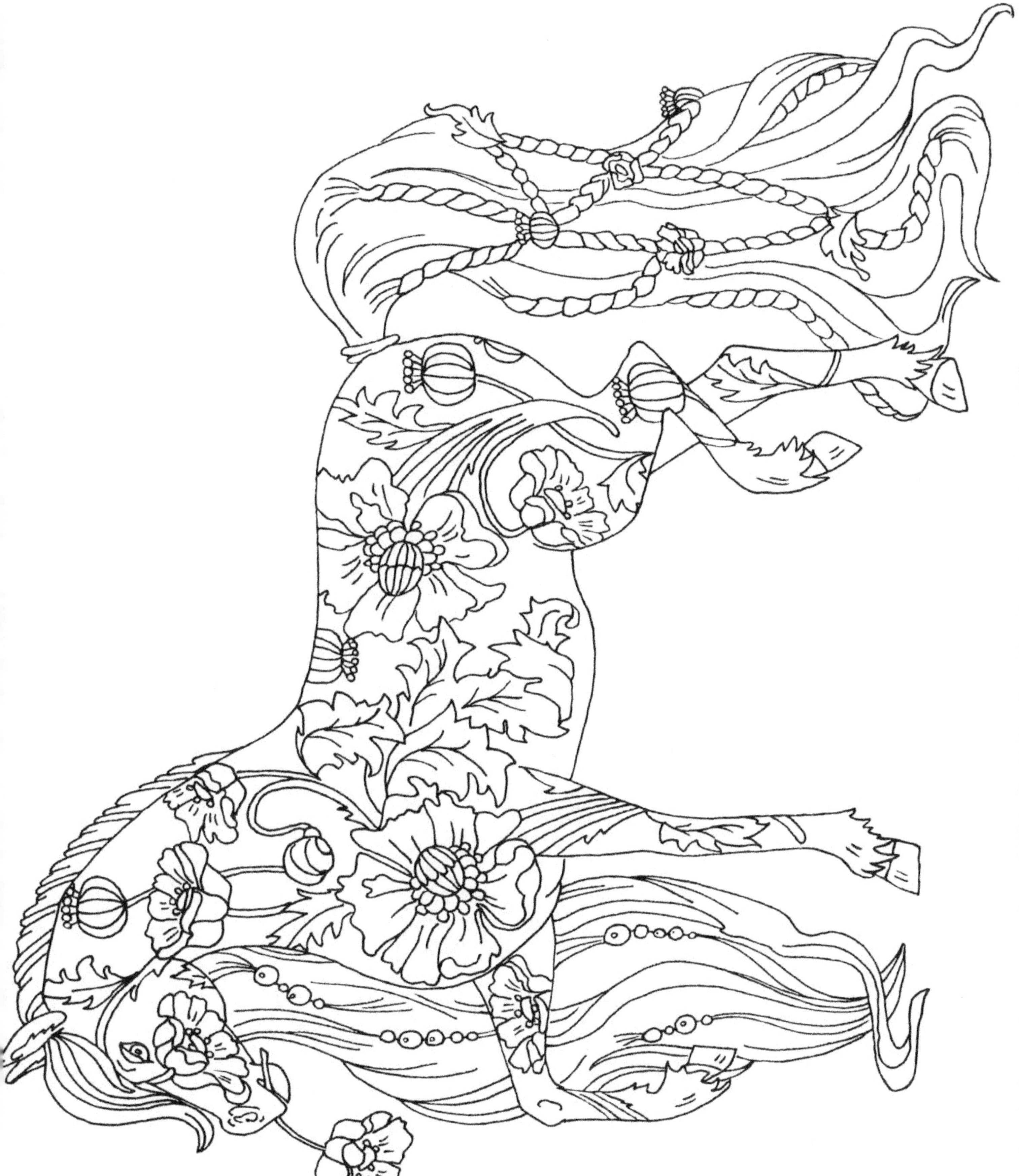

I'd appreciate it if you could leave a review on Amazon. Thank you!

www.ingramcontent.com/pod-product-compliance
Lightning Source LLC
Chambersburg PA
CBHW080612190526
45169CB00007B/2988
* 9 7 8 1 5 3 0 8 0 7 4 4 4 *